NICCOLÒ PAGANINI

24 CAPRICEN

für Violine / for Violin

Opus 1

Nach den Quellen herausgegeben von / Edited from the sources by

Klaus Hertel

ALLE RECHTE VORBEHALTEN · ALL RIGHTS RESERVED

EDITION PETERS

LEIPZIG · LONDON · NEW YORK

VORWORT

Niccolò Paganinis 24 Capricen zählen dank ihres melodischen Reichtums und der vielgestaltigen geigerischen Anforderungen, die von perpetuum-mobile-artigen Teilen über Doppelgriffpassagen in Terzen, Sexten, Oktaven und Dezimen bis hin zu mannigfaltigen bogentechnischen Effekten reichen, zu den berühmtesten Werken der Violinliteratur.

Ihr virtuoser Anspruch veranlaßte Schumann und Liszt, sie zu bravourösen Studienwerken für Klavier umzuarbeiten, andere Komponisten benutzten thematisches Material daraus zu eigenen Werken, so Szymanowski in seiner reizvollen Bearbeitung einiger Capricen für Violine und Klavier op. 40 und Rachmaninow in einer Rhapsodie für Klavier und Orchester op. 43.

Die vorliegende quellenkritische Neuausgabe basiert auf dem vom Verlag G. Ricordi, Mailand, 1984 herausgegebenen Faksimile-Druck des Autographs sowie der Erstausgabe von 1820, die unter dem Titel *24 Capricci per Violino solo ... op. 1* im gleichen Verlagshaus erschien, „gewidmet den Künstlern".

Mit * gekennzeichnete Stellen werden im Revisionsbericht, S. 63–66, erläutert.

Klaus Hertel

PREFACE

Owing to their melodic opulence and high violinistic standards, comprising perpetuum-mobile-like parts via double stop passages in thirds, sixths, octaves and tenths to manifold effects of the bowing, Niccolò Paganini's 24 Caprices represent some of the most popular works of the violin literature.

Their demand on virtuosity gave Schumann and Liszt rise to arrange them as brilliant study works for piano. Other composers used some thematic material from the caprices for their own works as, for instance, Szymanovski did in his charming adaptation of some Caprices for Violin and Piano, op. 40, and so did Rachmaninow in a Rhapsody for Piano and Orchestra, op. 43.

The present critical new edition is based on the facsimile of the autograph published by G. Ricordi, Milano, in 1984 as well as on the first edition of 1820, which was printed in the same publishing house under the title of *24 Capricci per Violino solo ... op. 1*, "dedicated to the artists".

Places marked with * are elucidated in the Editorial Notes, pp. 63–66.

Klaus Hertel

INHALT

24 CAPRICEN

I

Niccolò Paganini (1782-1840)
Opus 1
Herausgegeben von Klaus Hertel

II

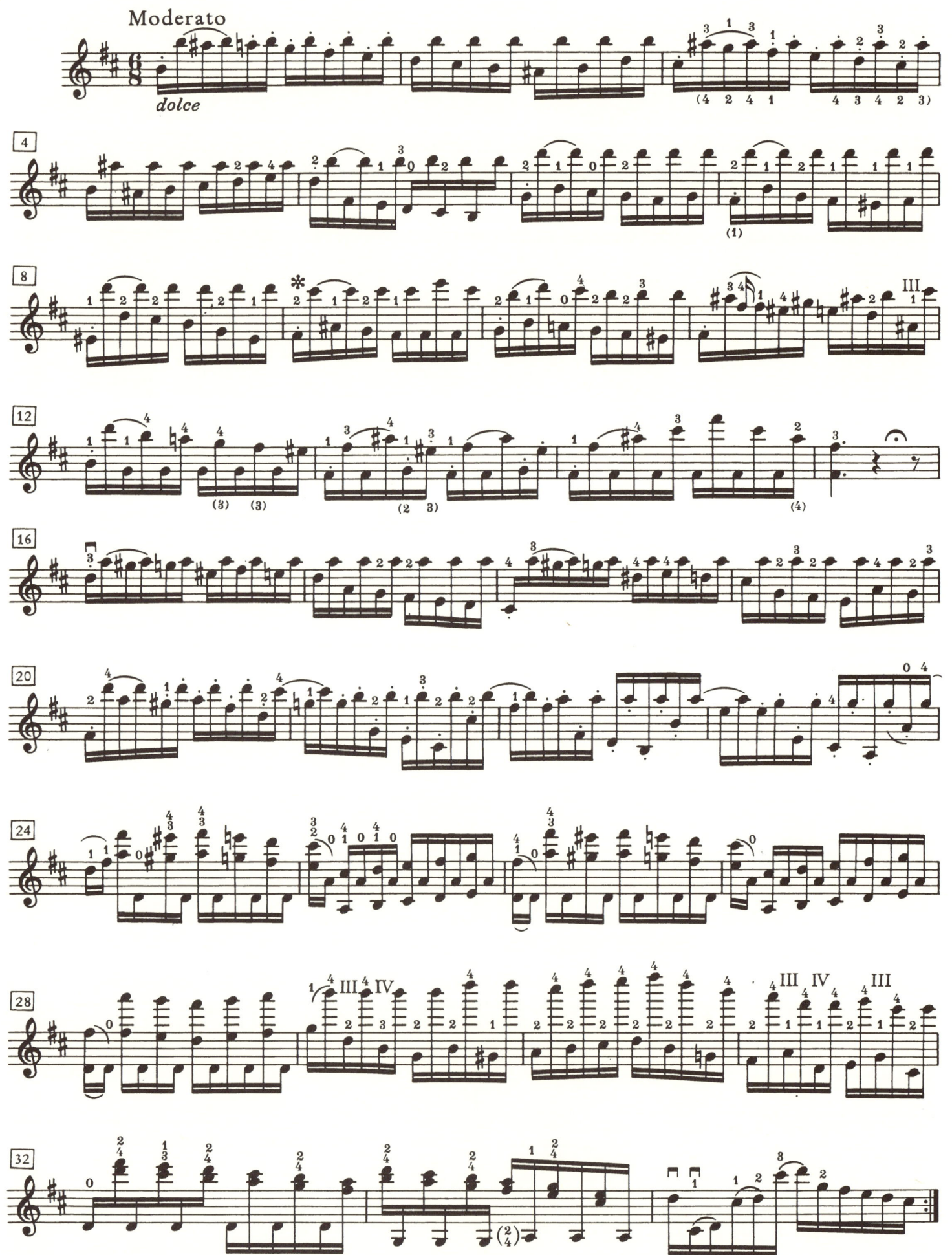

III

IV

VII

VIII

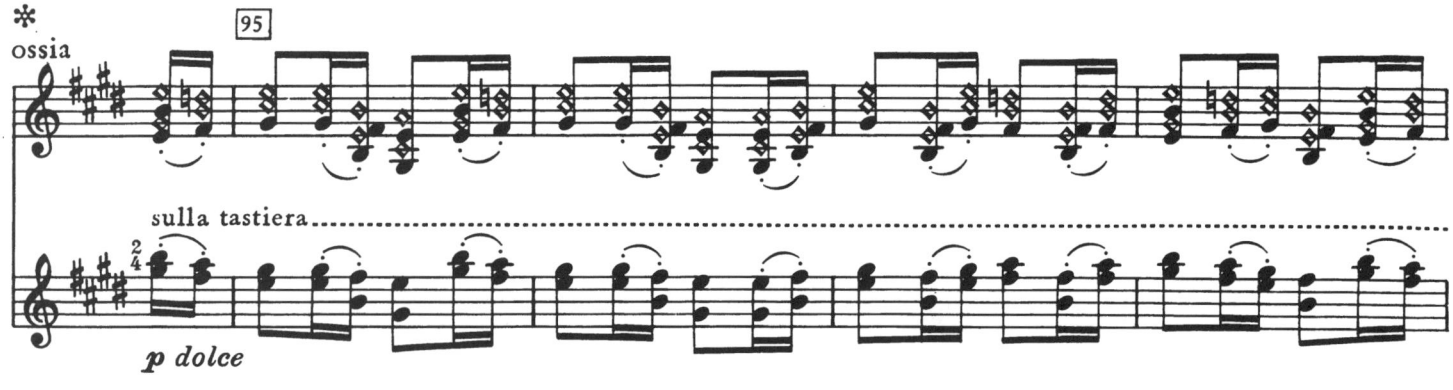

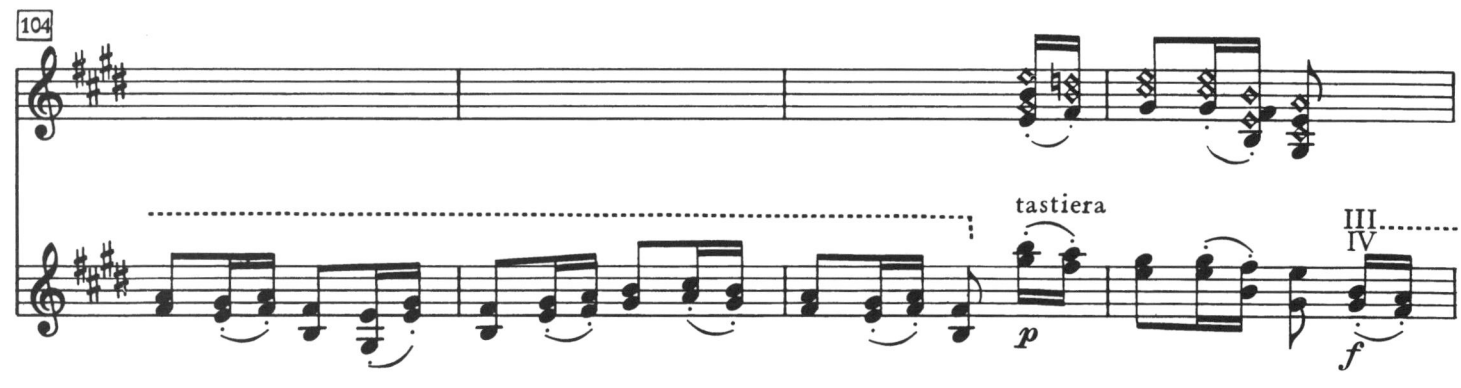

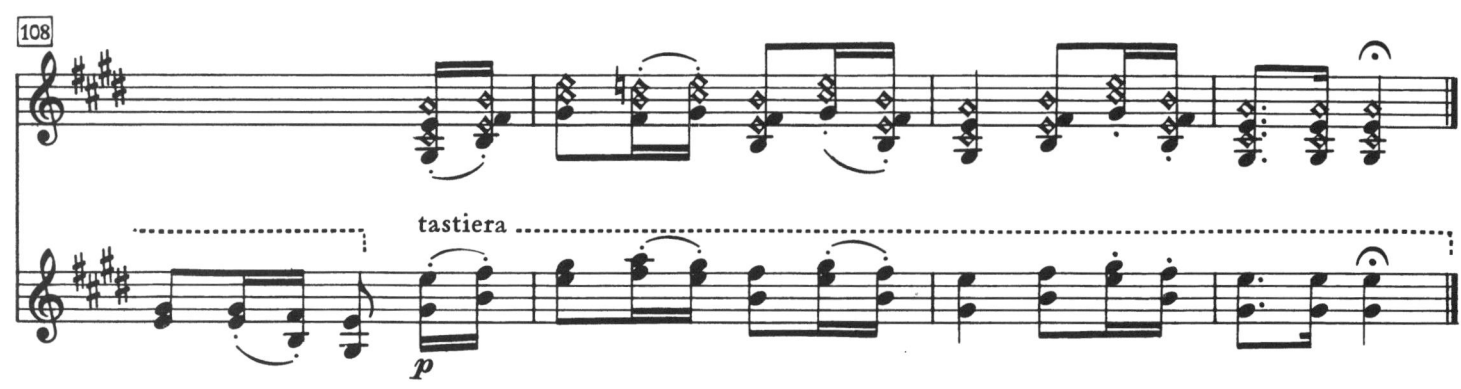

X

XI

XII

XIV

XV

XVI

XVIII

XIX

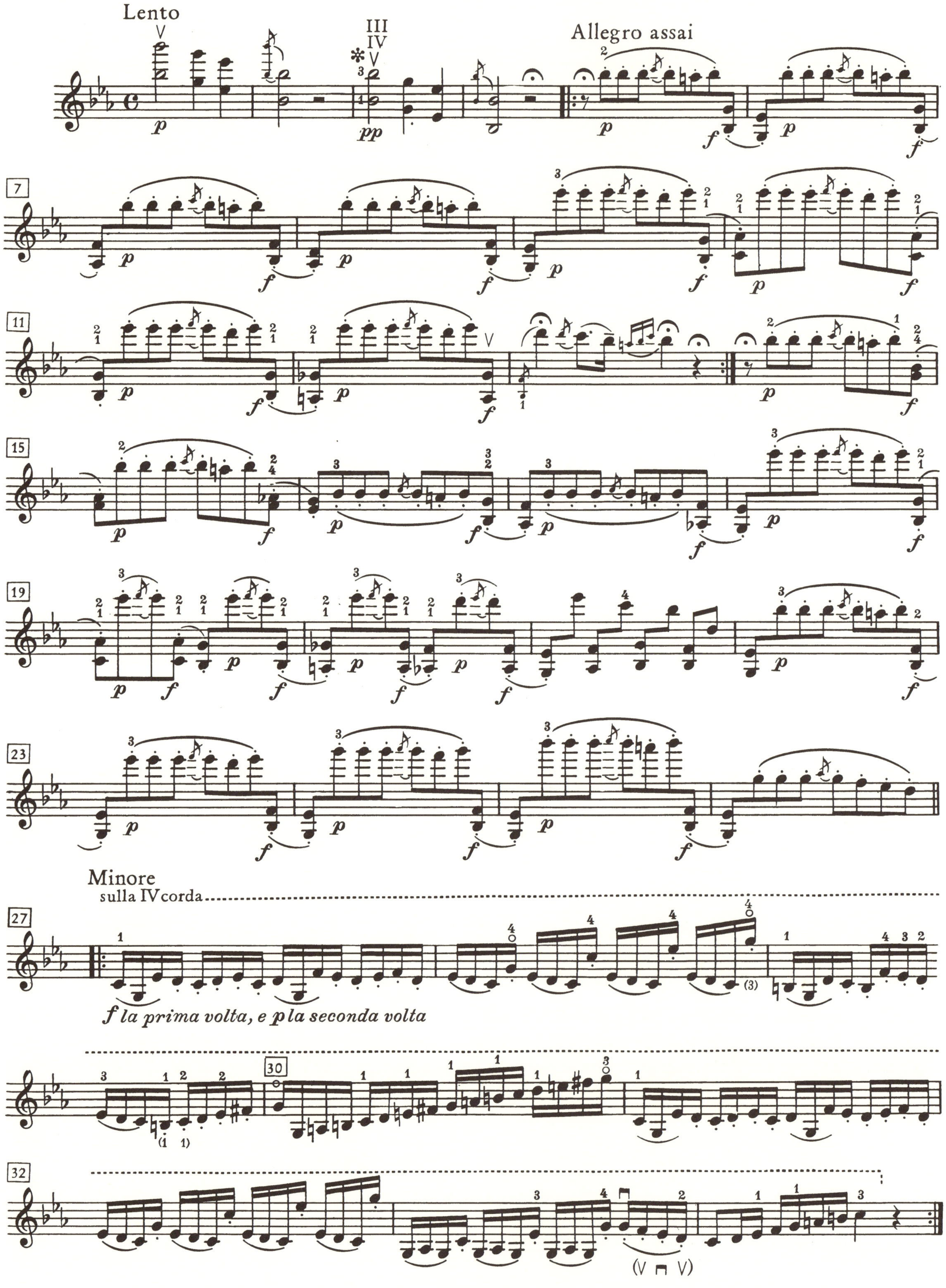
Lento
III
IV
Allegro assai
7
11
15
19
23
Minore
sulla IV corda
27
f la prima volta, e p la seconda volta
30
32

XX

XXI

XXII

XXIII

XXIV

EDITORIAL NOTES

The available Autograph (A) by Paganini is signified most precisely, but sparsely. Fingerings are given solely in the cadence-like introduction to No. 5, in the first bar and in bars 23–25 of Caprice No. 6 as well as in No. 2, where the composer several times marked the open string by a distinct 0.

As to the dynamics, many intensity marks have been proved to be added only to later editions. In order to proceed also in the present edition as faithfully as possible to the original, few additional dynamics, which the editor considered possible, are put into brackets.

Proposed alternatives to the phrasing are marked by dashed slurs. It should be pointed out that Paganini noted all trills to be played always without termination.

For an easier apperception of the rhythmic structure in Caprices Nos. 7, 9, 15, 23, and 24 the passage beams of the demisemiquavers were split up, and so were the beams of the sextuplets in Caprice No. 11.

Of all the instructions differing between the Autograph (A) and the First Edition (FE) those of the Autograph were preferred almost exclusively.

Detailed notes on the individual caprices:

No. 1

In b. 16 of A and FE both quavers are noted without slur; in b. 52 before E major begins again they are, however, noted with a slur. The slurred form would in any case require a small cut (caesura) for taking back the bow.

B. 44: Erroneously, in A and FE there is a minim rest. In bars 56/62/66 the semiquavers are each given with dots (thus performing them according to a certain bowing technique):

B. 75: As early as in FE, instead if g′ sharp–e′ (7th/8th notes and 15th/16th notes) b′–g′ sharp is noted. The Version of A is markedly easier to play with the otherwise necessary changes of position being omitted.

No. 2

B. 9: The tenth semiquaver is not noted as c′′′ sharp as it has been usually done since the FE (the compositional diction suggest that throughout always one part there is a melodic movement!).

B. 63: In all New Editions (NE) available and known to me an e′ sharp is given as the fifth semiquaver. In A and FE, however, a natural sign is clearly visible in front of this note.

No. 3

B. 108: The original notation of the sextuplet was realized according to bar 18 (two triplets).

No. 4

Bb. 12–15: Unlike FE, in A the quaver of the accompanying parts is noted without a subsequent dot. Thus, in my opinion, here also the conduct of part should differ from that in, for instance, bb. 51–53 or 62–64, respectively (the semiquaver rests were added by the editor).

B. 43: In A and FE, a flat sign is missing in front of the ninth semiquaver of the upper part (as the last semiquaver of the bar has in any case to be b′′ flat, this obviously is a slip). In harmonic respect the sequence follows from D major to G minor and C major to F minor.

T. 74: In A fehlt vor dem sechsten Sechzehntel der Oberstimme ein *b* (auch hier handelt es sich nach meiner Meinung um einen Notationsfehler). Auf Grund der melodischen Führung zum as'' des nächsten Taktes sollte auch hier unbedingt as'' gespielt werden.

T. 87: Beim dritten und vierten Sechzehntel ist nicht nur der im A und in der EA angegebene Wechsel zwischen Doppelgriff und Einstimmigkeit zu beachten, sondern vor allem auch der Unterschied zwischen Bindung und Noten mit Punkt.

T. 109: Auch in diesem Takt fehlen im A Auflösungszeichen vor der neunten Note bzw. vor den beiden Noten der letzten Zweiunddreißigstelgruppe (siehe auch Anmerkung zu Takt 43).

Nr. 5
T. 1: Die Bindungen der Anfangs- und Schlußkadenzen sind im A unterschiedlich angegeben, man wird sich voraussichtlich für eine der beiden aufgeführten Versionen entscheiden.

T. 31: Das in der EA erscheinende *b* (neuntes Sechzehntel) wurde in einer Reihe von NA übernommen.

Nr. 6
In den meisten NA wird die im A und in der EA vorgeschriebene Tempobezeichnung *Lento* durch *Adagio* ersetzt.

T. 48: Hier ist auf jeden Fall dem originalen Akzent auf dem dritten Viertel der Vorzug zu geben vor einem in den NA notierten Decrescendo.

Nr. 7
In den Takten 30/32/74 ist die exakte rhythmische Vorgabe des A und der EA jeweils

Offensichtlich wurde die heute übliche Spielweise mit durchgängigen Zweiunddreißigsteln aus Gründen des metrischen Gleichmaßes eingeführt.

T. 17: Ein Schreibfehler des A wurde auch in die EA übernommen, wo die dreizehnte Note als a'' notiert ist.

T. 74: Im A und der EA fehlt offensichtlich ein Kreuz vor der siebenten Note.

Nr. 8
T. 33: Es fehlt ein *b* vor dem d'' der letzten Sechzehntelgruppe, da in den Takten zuvor und danach nie eine übermäßige Quarte vorkommt. Vergleiche auch die Parallelstelle drei Takte nach Tonartwechsel!

T. 41: Entgegen dem A und der EA wurde in den NA d'' notiert.

T. 42: Entgegen dem A und der EA wurde in den NA als vorletzte Note der Unterstimme dis'' notiert.

T. 46: In A fehlt ein Auflösungszeichen vor der neunten Note der Unterstimme.

T. 48, 50: Entgegen A und EA wurde in den NA ein Auflösungszeichen vor as' bzw. as'' angegeben.

T. 52: In A und EA ist das dritte Sechzehntel einstimmig (nur f') notiert. Ich würde mich hier im Interesse des Fortgangs der Terzenführung für Doppelgriff d'-f' entscheiden. Ferner wurde in den NA entgegen dem A und der EA in den Takten 52/53 zum 13. Sechzehntel ges' in der Oberstimme angegeben.

T. 58: Seit der EA wird im Doppelgriff des vierten Viertels fälschlicherweise f' in der Oberstimme angegeben.

Nr. 9
T. 58/59: Entgegen dem A und der EA wurde in den NA anstelle f'' immer fis'' angegeben.

T. 95: Die Notation in Flageoletts steht nicht im A, sie stellt eine in NA hinzugefügte, aber sehr reizvolle Variante dar.

B. 74: In A, a flat sign is missing in front of the sixth semiquaver of the upper part (in my opinion, this again is a slip). As the melodic line leads to the a'' flat of the following bar, here also one should necessarily play a'' flat.

B. 87: As to the third and fourth semiquavers, not only the change between the double stop and the monophony, as it is indicated in A and FE, has to be taken into account, but also the difference between slurred notes with dots.

B. 109: Also in this bar of A the natural signs are missing in front of the ninth note and in front of the two notes of the last demisemiquaver group (cf. also note on b. 43).

No. 5
Bar 1: The slurs of the initial and final cadences in A are given differently; one probably has to decide on one of the two versions.

B. 31: The flat sign (ninth semiquaver) appearing in FE was also adopted ba a number of NE's.

No. 6
In most of the NE's the tempo designation *Lento* as it is given in A and FE is replaced by *Adagio*.

B. 48: Here the original accent on the third crotchet is in any case preferred to the decrescendo given in the NE's.

No. 7
In bb. 30/32/74 of both A and FE the exact rhythm is indicated minutely by

Today's common manner of playing throughout demisemiquavers has obviously been introduced for reasons of metric homogeneity.

B. 17: A slip in A was also adopted by FE where the thirteenth note is noted as a''.

B. 74: In A and FE there obviously is a sharp missing in front of the seventh note.

No. 8
B. 33: A flat is missing in front of the d'' of the last semiquaver group, since in the bars preceding and following it there never occurs an augmented fourth. Cf. also the parallel place 3 bars after the change of the key!

B. 41: Unlike A and FE, in the NE's d'' is noted.

B. 42: Unlike A and FE, in the NE's the last but one note of the lower voice is noted as d'' sharp.

B. 46: A natural sign is missing in A in front of the ninth note of the lower voice.

B. 48 and 50: Unlike A and FE, in NE's a natural sign is noted in front of a flat.

Bar 52: In A and FE, the third semiquaver is noted solely as f'. In my opinion, for continuing the conduct in thirds one should decide on the double stop d'-f'. Besides, unlike A and FE, in NE's in bars 52/53 g' flat is noted in the upper voice to the 13th semiquaver.

Bar 58: Since FE, in the double stop of the fourth crotchet f' is erroneously given in the upper voice.

No. 9
Bars 58/59: Unlike A and FE, in NE's f'' sharp is always noted for f''.

B. 95: The notation in flageolets is not found in A; it is a most charming variant, added to later editions.

Nr. 10

In T. 4–6 stehen im A und in der EA noch ganztaktige Bögen zusätzlich notiert.

T. 30: In A und EA stehen keine Auflösungszeichen vor den b-Noten, jedoch würde ich mich hier für den harmonischen Hintergrund B^7–Es-Dur, G^7–c-Moll entscheiden und demzufolge h spielen.

T. 49: Entgegen dem A und der EA wurde in den NA das Auflösungszeichen bereits vor der zweiten Note geschrieben, wo jedoch noch cis'' zu spielen ist.

Nr. 11

T. 29: In A und EA ist der gesamte Presto-Teil ohne Bindebögen notiert.

T. 97: Hier ist ein Schreibfehler des A auch in die EA übernommen worden (im zweiten Viertel muß es in der Unterstimme nicht e^1 sondern f^1 heißen; siehe auch Parallelstelle Takt 23).

Nr. 12

T. 52: In A und EA ist vor der achten Note ein *b* notiert. Allerdings weist die Parallelstelle, T. 42 d''–gis' aus, also eine verminderte Quinte. Sollte Paganini hier anstelle eines Auflösungszeichens versehentlich ein *b* geschrieben haben?

T. 58: Im A und EA fehlt vor der drittletzten Note ein Auflösungszeichen, da an den gleichlautenden Stellen immer eine verminderte Duodezime ablesbar ist (siehe T. 15, 16, 34, 35, 44, 45, 59).

Nr. 13

T. 36: Entgegen dem A und der EA wurde in den NA die achte Note immer als e' angegeben.

Nr. 14

Zwei offensichtliche Schreibfehler wurden vom A in die EA übernommen:

T. 16: Es fehlt ein Kreuz in A und EA vor der Note f^1 (siehe vorhergehende und nachfolgende Takte).

T. 36: Hier ist beim zweiten Viertel in A und EA die Note h' nicht notiert, mit Sicherheit vergessen (Sequenzform!).

Nr. 16

T. 17: In A und EA fehlt ein Auflösungszeichen vor der letzten Note (zwei Takte später, in der oberen Oktave, ist es notiert).

Nr. 17

Im Minore stehen in A und EA in den Takten 24, 27 und 28 vor der letzten Note keine Auflösungszeichen (bestimmt soll die Figur aber immer wie im Takt 23 gespielt werden). Ebenso fehlt im Takt 26 ein *b* vor der fünften und vor der neunten Note, adäquat dem Takt 30.

Nr. 18

T. 38: Das Auflösungszeichen ist im A und in der EA schon vor der Note c'' notiert, wo es keinerlei Sinn hat. Offensichtlich ist es eine Note zu früh angebracht.

Nr. 19

T. 3: A und EA notieren nur b''.

Nr. 20

T. 17: In EA sind die drei letzten Achtel falsch notiert (analog den drei Achteln in Takt 18).

T. 26: In A und EA fehlt *tr*.

Nr. 21

T. 24: Hier, wie 6 Takte später in der Oktavierung, wird, entgegen der Notation im A bzw. EA in den NA his in der Unterstimme angegeben.

Nr. 22

T. 39: Hier hat sich fälschlicherweise in den NA ein cis'' und cis' (6. und 11. Note) „eingeschlichen"; A und EA weisen ein klares c aus.

Nr. 23

T. 27: In A und EA ist als viertletztes Zweiunddreißigstel as^1 notiert; in Angleichung an die zwei ersten Fünftongruppen in T. 28 wäre durchaus ein g' vertretbar.

No. 10

In bb. 4 to 6 of A and FE additional slurs are noted over the entire bars.

B. 30: In A and FE there is no natural sign in front of b flat. Nevertheless, I should decide on the harmonic background of B flat^7–E flat major–G^7–C minor, thus playing b.

B. 49: Unlike A and FE, in the NE's the natural sign is noted already in front of the second note where, however, still c'' sharp has to be played.

No. 11

B. 29: In A the entire Presto section is noted without slurs.

B. 97: A slip in A was also adopted by FE (in the lower part the second crotchet has to be f, not e; cf. also parallel place in bar 23).

No. 12

B. 52: In A and FE a flat sign is noted in front of the eighth note. The parallel place in b. 42, however, shows d''–g' sharp, i.e. a diminished fifth. Had Paganini here probably written by mistake a flat sign instead of a natural one?

B. 58: In A and FE a natural sign is missing in front of the last but two note, since there always is a diminished twelfth in parallel places (cf. bb. 15, 16, 34, 35, 44, 45, 59).

No. 13

Bar 36: Unlike A and FE, in the NE's the eighth note is always noted as e'.

No. 14

Two obvious slips in A were adopted by FE.

B. 16: A sharp sign is missing in front of F (see preceding and following bars).

B. 36: The B in the second crotchet is missing, slurely forgotten (sequential form).

No. 16

B. 17: In A and FE a natural sign is missing in front of the last note (two bars later it is noted in the upper octave).

No. 17

In bb. 24, 27, and 28 of the Minore section of A and FE there are no natural signs in front of the last note (but most certainly is the figure to be played like in b. 23). Natural signs are missing also in b. 26 in front of the fifth and ninth notes, adequate to b. 30.

No. 18

B. 38: In A and FE the natural sign is noted already before c'' where it is senseless. It has obviously been placed one note too early.

No. 19

B. 3: A and FE only b'' flat.

No. 20

B. 17: In FE last three quavers are wrongly noted (by analogy with the three quavers in b. 18).

B. 26: In A and FE *tr* is missing.

No. 21

B. 24: Unlike A and FE, in the NE's in this bar as also in the transpositions by one octave 6 bars later, b sharp is given in the lower voice.

No. 22

B. 39: c sharp (6th and 11th notes) has erroneously entered the NE's; A and FE clearly point out c.

No. 23

B. 27: In A and FE, A flat is noted as the last but three demisemiquaver; on the analogy of the first two five-tone groups in bar 28' g would be acceptable.

T. 29: Entgegen A und EA steht in den NA vor der dritten Note ein Auflösungszeichen.

T. 32: Die fünfte Note muß laut A f′ sein; bereits in der EA erscheint dafür as′.

Nr. 24

T. 89: Entgegen A und EA steht in den NA ein *b* vor der vorletzten Note.

T. 97: In A sind für diese Variation ganztaktige Bindungen angegeben.

T. 115: Als Variante sollte hier folgende Ausführung möglich sein:

T. 152–155: Es wurde eine Angleichung der Notation an die tatsächlichen rhythmischen Werte vorgenommen.

B. 29: Unlike A and FE, in the NE's there is a natural sign in front of the third note.

Bar: 32: According to A, the fifth note has to be f′; but as early as in FE, however, a′ flat appears instead.

No. 24

B. 89: Unlike A and FE, in the NE's there is a flat in front of the last but one note.

B. 97: In A, one-bar slurs are given for this variation.

B. 115: A variant of performing migth be as follows

Bb. 152 to 155: The notation has been adapted to the true rhythmic values.